TRUMPET & BARITONE T.C.

From The Baroque To The 20th Century

Classical Trios for All

Playable on ANY THREE INSTRUMENTS
or any number of instruments in ensemble

WILLIAM RYDEN

TABLE OF CONTENTS

INSTRUMENTATION

EL96139 - Piano/Conductor, Oboe
EL96140 - Flute, Piccolo
EL96141 - Bb Clarinet, Bass Clarinet
EL96142 - Alto Saxophone
  (Eb Saxes and Eb Clarinets)
EL96143 - Tenor Saxophone
EL96144 - Bb Trumpet, Baritone T.C.

EL96145 - Horn in F
EL96146 - Trombone,
  Baritone B.C., Bassoon, Tuba
EL96147 - Violin
EL96148 - Viola
EL96149 - Cello/Bass
EL96150 - Percussion

Editor: Thom Proctor
Cover: Dallas Soto

ALPHABETICAL CONTENTS

WILLIAM RYDEN was born in New York City and is a life-long resident of Forest Hills, New York. He received his advanced musical training at The American Conservatory of Music in Chicago and at the Mannes College of Music in New York. The diversity of his composing ranges from solos to orchestra works, in both vocal and instrumental music. Since 1982 he has received 25 grants from the Meet-the-Composer Foundation. His numerous compositions and arrangements have been published by various prominent educational and performance music publishers.

THE VILLAGE MAIDEN

B♭ TRUMPET/BARITONE T.C.

JEAN PHILLIPE RAMEAU
(1683-1764)

ROSAMUNDE

Entr'acte No. 2, D.797

FRANZ SCHUBERT
(1797-1828)

GERMAN DANCE
WoO 13, No. 2

LUDWIG VAN BEETHOVEN
(1770-1827)

Allegro moderato

D.C. al Fine

LÄNDLER
Austrian Dance

FRANZ SCHUBERT
(1797-1828)

Andante con moto

ROMANCE
Album for the Young, Opus 68, No. 19

ROBERT SCHUMANN
(1810-1856)

Moderato con moto

RIGAUDON

LOUIS CLAUDE DAQUIN
(1694-1772)

PASSACAGLIA
"Dido and Aeneas"

HENRY PURCELL
(1659-1695)

Larghetto

TRIO in F
Minuet, BWV 820

JOHANN SEBASTIAN BACH
(1685-1750)

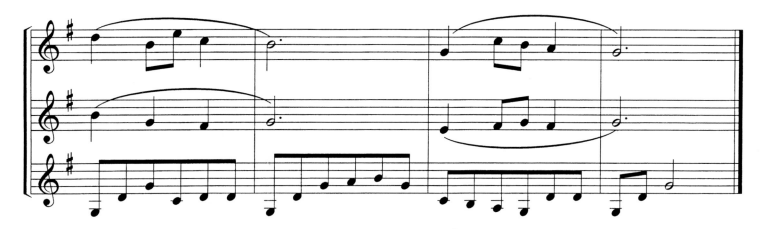

ANDANTINO

DANIEL GOTTLOB TÜRK
(1750-1813)

CANON

ANTONIO CALDARA
(1670-1736)

WALTZ
"Eugen Onegin"

PIOTR ILYICH TCHAIKOVSKY
(1840-1893)

Fast waltz tempo

MARCH
"La Diva de L'empire"
(1919)

ERIK SATIE
(1866-1925)

2. Play second time only.

Fine

D.S. % al Fine

Minuet

Hob. XVI, No. 5

JOSEPH HAYDN
(1732-1809)

EL96144

WALTZ
in B minor
Opus 39, No. 11

JOHANNES BRAHMS
(1833-1897)

ADAGIO
Sonata, Opus 1, No. 3

ARCANGELO CORELLI
(1653-1713)